Circus

Circus Clowns

Denise M. Jordan

Heinemann Library
Chicago, Illinois

Customer Service 888-454-2279
Visit our website at www.heinemannlibrary.com

Designed by Sue Emerson, Heinemann Library
Printed and bound in the U.S.A. by Lake Book

06 05 04 03
10 9 8 7 6 5 4 3 2

Library of Congress Cataloging-in-Publication Data
Jordan, Denise M.
   Circus clowns / Denise Jordan.
      p. cm. — (Circus)
Includes index.
Summary: Introduces the world of circus clowns and the kind of acts they perform.
   ISBN: 1-58810-544-X (HC), 1-58810-752-3 (Pbk.)
   1. Clowns—Juvenile literature. [1. Clowns. 2. Circus performers.] I. Title.
   GV1828 .J67 2002
   791.3'3—dc21

2001004792

Acknowledgments
The author and publishers are grateful to the following for permission to reproduce copyright material:
p. 4 Aneal Vohra/Unicorn Stock Photos; pp. 5, 13, 19 Greg Williams/Heinemann Library; p. 6 Earl & Nazima Kowall/ Corbis; pp. 7, 20 Scott McKiernan/ZUMA Press; p. 8 N & J Wiseman/Trip; p. 9 MacDonald Photography/Unicorn Stock Photos; p. 10 Bettmann/Corbis; p. 11 Masha Nordbye/Bruce Coleman Inc.; p. 12 Roland Raith; pp. 14, 16 Joel Dexter/ Unicorn Stock Photos; pp. 15, 22 Eugene G. Schulz; p. 17 Layne Kennedy/Corbis; p. 18L H. Gariety/Trip; p. 18R Chuck Fishman/Contact Press Images/PictureQuest; p. 21 National Geographic Society

Cover photograph courtesy of Greg Williams/Heinemann Library

Every effort has been made to contact copyright holders of any material reproduced in this book. Any omissions will be rectified in subsequent printings if notice is given to the publisher.

Special thanks to our advisory panel for their help in the preparation of this book:

Eileen Day, Preschool Teacher
Chicago, IL

Paula Fischer, K–1 Teacher
Indianapolis, IN

Sandra Gilbert,
Library Media Specialist
Houston, TX

Angela Leeper,
Educational Consultant
North Carolina Department
of Public Instruction
Raleigh, NC

Pam McDonald, Reading Teacher
Winter Springs, FL

Melinda Murphy,
Library Media Specialist
Houston, TX

Helen Rosenberg, MLS
Chicago, IL

Anna Marie Varakin,
Reading Instructor
Western Maryland College

The publishers would also like to thank Fred Dahlinger, Jr., Director of Collections and Research at the Circus World Museum in Baraboo, Wisconsin, and Smita Parida for their help in reviewing the contents of this book.

Some words are shown in bold, **like this.**
You can find them in the picture glossary on page 23.

Contents

What Are Clowns?

Clowns are people who do funny things.

Clowns wear funny clothes.

Clowns make people laugh.

You can see clowns at the circus.

When Do People See Clowns?

Clowns race into the **ring** when the circus starts.

While circus acts change, clowns
do funny things.

Clowns keep people laughing.

What Do Clowns Do?

Clowns play jokes on other clowns.

They do magic tricks and **juggle**.

Some clowns ride **unicycles.**

What Animals Help Clowns?

Circus clowns work with many kinds of animals.

Some clowns work with dogs.

Other clowns work with cats.

The clowns teach the animals to do funny things, too.

Why Don't Clowns Talk?

Some people sit far away from the **ring**.

It is hard to hear.

Clowns are funny without talking.

What Do Clowns Wear?

Clowns paint their faces.

They paint big, red mouths.

wig

Clowns wear **wigs.**

They have baggy clothes and silly shoes.

Where Do Circus Clowns Dress?

Clown alley is a special place for clowns.

It is where clowns put on their makeup.

It is where clowns keep their clothes.

What Kinds of Clowns Are There?

Auguste clowns wear colorful clothes and makeup.

Whiteface clowns wear black and white.

Character clowns dress up like police officers or cowboys.

How Do People Learn to Be Clowns?

Some clowns grow up in the circus.

Some circus families teach their children to be clowns.

There are clown schools, too.

People can learn to be clowns.

Quiz

What are these clown things?

Can you find them in the book?

Look for the answers on page 24.

?

?

Picture Glossary

auguste clown
(oh-GOOST klown)
page 18

ring
pages 6, 12

character clown
(KAIR-ik-ter
klown)
page 19

unicycle
page 9

clown alley
page 16

**whiteface
clown**
page 18

juggle
page 8

wig
page 15

Note to Parents and Teachers

Reading for information is an important part of a child's literacy development. Learning begins with a question about something. Help children think of themselves as investigators and researchers by encouraging their questions about the world around them. Each chapter in this book begins with a question. Read the question together. Look at the pictures. Talk about what you think the answer might be. Then read the text to find out if your predictions were correct. Think of other questions you could ask about the topic, and discuss where you might find the answers. Assist children in using the picture glossary and the index to practice new vocabulary and research skills.

Index

Answers to quiz on page 22

wig

silly shoes